Cooking for Kids
WINNING RECIPES

Publications International, Ltd.
Favorite Brand Name Recipes at www.fbnr.com

Pictured on the front cover *(left to right):* Spotted Butterfly Sandwich *(page 50),* Cookie Dough Bears *(page 122),* Happy Clown Face *(page 88),* Cookie Caterpillars *(page 120),* Giggle Jiggle Parfaits *(page 128),* Mini Pickle Sea Monster Burgers *(page 102),* Little Piggy Pies *(page 108)* and Happy-Face Kids' Pizza *(page 100).*

Pictured on the back cover *(top to bottom):* Breakfast Mice *(page 18)* and Turkey Bacon Mini Wafflewiches *(page 66).*

ISBN-13: 978-1-4127-9794-8
ISBN-10: 1-4127-9794-2

Library of Congress Control Number: 2009924021

Manufactured in China.

8 7 6 5 4 3 2 1

Microwave Cooking: Microwave ovens vary in wattage. Use the cooking times as guidelines and check for doneness before adding more time.

Preparation/Cooking Times: Preparation times are based on the approximate amount of time required to assemble the recipe before cooking, baking, chilling or serving. These times include preparation steps such as measuring, chopping and mixing. The fact that some preparations and cooking can be done simultaneously is taken into account. Preparation of optional ingredients and serving suggestions is not included.

Table of Contents

Rise & Shine

Puffy Pancake

3 tablespoons melted butter, divided
½ cup all-purpose flour
½ cup milk
2 eggs
¼ teaspoon salt
2 bananas, sliced
1 cup sliced strawberries
2 tablespoons chocolate syrup
   Powdered sugar (optional)

1. Preheat oven to 400°F. Pour 2 tablespoons butter into large ovenproof skillet; brush onto side of skillet.

2. Combine flour, milk, eggs, remaining 1 tablespoon butter and salt in medium bowl; whisk 1 minute. Pour batter into prepared skillet.

3. Bake 20 to 22 minutes or until pancake is golden brown and puffed up side of skillet. Remove from oven and immediately fill with fruit. Drizzle with chocolate syrup; sprinkle with powdered sugar, if desired.

Makes 4 servings

Note: This pancake can also be prepared in a deep-dish pie plate.

Blueberry Cinnamon Muffins

1¼ cups all-purpose flour
½ cup **CREAM OF WHEAT®** Cinnamon Swirl Instant Hot Cereal,
   uncooked
½ cup sugar, divided
1 tablespoon baking powder
2 teaspoons ground cinnamon
½ teaspoon salt
1 cup milk
1 egg
2 tablespoons oil
1 teaspoon vanilla extract
1 cup fresh or frozen blueberries
2 tablespoons apple juice

1. Preheat oven to 400°F. Grease 12 (2½-inch) muffin cups. Mix flour, Cream of Wheat, ¼ cup sugar, baking powder, cinnamon and salt in medium bowl; set aside.

2. Beat milk, egg, oil and vanilla with wire whisk in separate bowl until well blended. Add to dry ingredients; stir just until moistened. Gently stir in blueberries. Spoon evenly into prepared muffin cups, filling each cup two-thirds full.

3. Bake 18 to 20 minutes or until toothpick inserted into centers comes out clean. Remove muffins from pan.

4. Brush tops of warm muffins with apple juice; roll in remaining ¼ cup sugar. Serve warm.   *Makes 12 muffins*

Variation: To make Strawberries 'n Cream Muffins, use CREAM OF WHEAT® Strawberries 'n Cream Instant Hot Cereal and frozen strawberries.

Prep Time: 10 minutes • **Start to Finish Time:** 30 minutes

Blueberry Cinnamon Muffins

Bacon and Egg Cups

12 slices bacon, cut crosswise into thirds
6 eggs
½ cup diced bell pepper
½ cup shredded pepper jack cheese
½ cup half-and-half
¼ teaspoon salt
¼ teaspoon black pepper

1. Preheat oven to 350°F. Lightly spray 12 standard (2½-inch) muffin cups with nonstick cooking spray.

2. Arrange bacon slices flat in single layers on plates lined with paper towels. Do not overlap. Top with additional sheets of paper towels. Microwave on HIGH 2 to 3 minutes or until cooked yet pliable. Place 3 bacon slices in each cup, overlapping in bottom of each prepared muffin cup.

3. Beat eggs, bell pepper, cheese, half-and-half, salt and black pepper in medium bowl until well blended. Fill each muffin cup with ¼ cup egg mixture. Bake 20 to 25 minutes or until eggs are set in center. Run knife around edge of each cup before removing from pan.

Makes 12 servings

 *Kitchen Tip*

To save time, look for mixed diced bell peppers in the produce section of the grocery store.

Bacon & Egg Cups

Toll House® Mini Morsel Pancakes

2½ cups all-purpose flour
  1 cup (6 ounces) NESTLÉ® TOLL HOUSE® Semi-Sweet Chocolate
    Mini Morsels
  1 tablespoon baking powder
  ½ teaspoon salt
1¾ cups milk
  2 large eggs
  ⅓ cup vegetable oil
  ⅓ cup packed brown sugar
    Powdered sugar
    Fresh sliced strawberries (optional)
    Maple syrup

COMBINE flour, morsels, baking powder and salt in large bowl. Combine milk, eggs, vegetable oil and brown sugar in medium bowl; add to flour mixture. Stir just until moistened (batter may be lumpy).

HEAT griddle or skillet over medium heat; brush lightly with vegetable oil. Pour ¼ cup of batter onto hot griddle; cook until bubbles begin to burst. Turn; continue to cook for about 1 minute longer or until golden. Repeat with remaining batter.

SPRINKLE with powdered sugar; top with strawberries. Serve with maple syrup.   *Makes about 18 pancakes*

Toll House® Mini Morsel Pancakes

Breakfast Tacos

6 mini taco shells *or* 2 regular-sized taco shells
2 eggs
   Nonstick cooking spray
½ teaspoon taco seasoning mix
2 tablespoons shredded Cheddar cheese or cheese sauce
2 tablespoons mild salsa
2 tablespoons chopped fresh parsley
   Sliced green onion and shredded lettuce (optional)

1. Heat taco shells according to package directions; cool slightly. Meanwhile, beat eggs in small bowl until well blended. Spray small skillet with cooking spray; heat over medium-low heat.

2. Pour eggs into skillet; cook and stir until desired doneness. Sprinkle taco seasoning mix over eggs.

3. Spoon egg mixture into taco shells. Top each taco with 1 teaspoon *each* cheese, salsa and parsley. Add green onion and lettuce, if desired.

Makes 2 servings

Hawaiian Breakfast Pizza

2 teaspoons pineapple jam or barbecue sauce
1 English muffin, split in half and toasted
1 slice (1 ounce) smoked ham, diced
½ cup pineapple tidbits, drained
2 tablespoons shredded Cheddar cheese

1. Spread jam over each muffin half; place on foil-lined toaster oven tray. Sprinkle ham and pineapple tidbits over muffin halves; top with cheese.

2. Toast about 2 minutes or until cheese is melted.

Makes 1 serving

Note: To heat in a conventional oven, preheat oven to 400°F. Heat muffins on a foil-lined baking sheet about 5 minutes or until cheese is melted.

Breakfast Tacos

Deep-Dish Breakfast Pizza

1 cup shredded mozzarella cheese (about 4 ounces)
1 cup shredded Cheddar cheese (about 4 ounces)
1 pound breakfast or sweet Italian sausage links, removed
    from casings and crumbled
1 small red bell pepper, diced
1 small onion, chopped
1 cup RAGÚ® Old World Style® Pasta Sauce
1 container (13.8 ounces) refrigerated pizza crust dough
4 eggs, lightly beaten

1. Preheat oven to 400°F. In medium bowl, combine mozzarella and Cheddar cheese; set aside.

2. In 12-inch nonstick skillet, cook sausage, red pepper and onion over medium-high heat, stirring occasionally, 5 minutes or until sausage is browned; drain. Stir in Pasta Sauce and simmer 2 minutes.

3. Meanwhile, press pizza dough into bottom and 2 inches up sides of 13×9-inch baking pan; sprinkle with ½ of the cheese mixture. Evenly spoon sausage mixture over cheese, then pour in eggs. Bake 20 minutes. Top with remaining cheese mixture and bake an additional 5 minutes or until cheese is melted and eggs in center are set.

Makes 8 servings

Prep Time: 15 minutes • Cook Time: 32 minutes

Breakfast Banana Split

1 banana
3 strawberries, sliced
¼ cup fresh blueberries
1 container (6 ounces) strawberry yogurt "fruit on the bottom,"
    stirred
1 tablespoon granola
1 maraschino cherry

1. Peel banana; cut in half lengthwise. Place banana in serving dish and separate halves. Top with half of strawberries and blueberries.

2. Gently spoon yogurt over berries. Top with remaining berries; sprinkle with granola. Garnish with cherry.   *Makes 1 serving*

Prep Time: 5 minutes

Kid's Favorite Chocolate Chip Muffins

1½ cups all-purpose flour
1½ cups whole wheat flour
2 teaspoons baking soda
2 teaspoons baking powder
2 teaspoons ground cinnamon or pumpkin pie spice
½ teaspoon salt
4 large eggs, slightly beaten
2 cups granulated sugar
1 can (15 ounces) LIBBY'S® 100% Pure Pumpkin
1 cup vegetable oil
2 cups (12-ounce package) NESTLÉ® TOLL HOUSE® Semi-Sweet
    Chocolate Morsels

PREHEAT oven to 350°F. Grease 36 (2½-inch) muffin cups or line with paper bake cups.

COMBINE all-purpose flour, whole wheat flour, baking soda, baking powder, cinnamon and salt in medium bowl. Combine eggs and sugar in large bowl. Add pumpkin and oil; mix well. Stir in flour mixture until moistened. Stir in morsels. Spoon batter into prepared muffin cups.

BAKE for 20 to 25 minutes or until top springs back when lightly touched. Cool in pans on wire racks for 5 minutes; remove from pans.
                              Makes 3 dozen muffins

Brown Sugar and Cinnamon Pancakes

½ cup all-purpose flour
½ packet CREAM OF WHEAT® Maple Brown Sugar Instant Hot
    Cereal, uncooked
½ packet CREAM OF WHEAT® Cinnamon Swirl Instant Hot
    Cereal,* uncooked
1 tablespoon baking powder
1 cup milk
1 egg
2 tablespoons margarine or butter, melted
    Additional butter (optional)
    MAPLE GROVE FARMS® of Vermont Pure Maple Syrup
    (optional)

Or substitute CREAM OF WHEAT® Apples 'n Cinnamon Instant Hot Cereal.

1. Mix flour, Cream of Wheat cereals and baking powder in medium bowl; set aside.

2. Beat milk, egg and margarine in separate bowl with wire whisk until well blended. Add to dry ingredients; mix just until blended. Let stand 5 minutes.

3. Coat hot griddle or hot skillet with nonstick cooking spray. Ladle scant ¼ cup batter onto griddle for each pancake. Cook until bubbles form on top; turn over and cook until lightly browned. Repeat with remaining pancake batter. Serve with butter and maple syrup, if desired.   *Makes 8 pancakes*

Prep Time: 15 minutes • **Start to Finish Time:** 30 minutes

Kitchen Tip

Make sure the griddle is hot before using. Flick
a few drops of water onto the surface; if the
water sizzles, the griddle is ready.

Brown Sugar and Cinnamon Pancakes

Breakfast Mice

2 hard-cooked eggs, peeled and halved lengthwise
2 teaspoons mayonnaise
¼ teaspoon salt
2 radishes, thinly sliced and root ends reserved
8 raisins or currants
1 ounce Cheddar cheese, shredded or cubed
    Spinach or lettuce leaves (optional)

1. Gently scoop egg yolks into small bowl. Mash yolks, mayonnaise and salt until smooth. Spoon yolk mixture back into egg halves. Place 2 halves, cut side down, on each serving plate.

2. Cut two tiny slits near the narrow end of each egg half; position 2 radish slices on each half for ears. Use the root end of each radish to form tails. Push raisins into each egg half to form eyes. Place small pile of cheese in front of each mouse. Garnish with spinach leaves, if desired.   *Makes 2 servings*

Editor's Note

Brighten your kids' morning with these cute little mice for breakfast. You can conveniently hard-cook the eggs and make the yolk mixture the night before. Then simply decorate the mice in the morning and watch the smiles light up your kids' faces.

Breakfast Mice

Apple and Cheese Pockets

2 cups Golden Delicious apples, peeled, cored and finely
 chopped (about 2 medium)
2 cups shredded sharp Cheddar cheese
2 tablespoons apple jelly
¼ teaspoon curry powder
1 package (about 16 ounces) large refrigerated biscuits (8 biscuits)

1. Preheat oven to 350°F. Line baking sheet with parchment paper.

2. Combine apples, cheese, jelly and curry powder in large bowl; stir well.

3. Roll out 1 biscuit on lightly floured surface to 6½-inch circle.
Place ½ cup apple mixture in center. Fold biscuit over filling to form
semicircle; press to seal tightly. Place on baking sheet. Repeat with
remaining biscuits and filling. Bake 15 to 18 minutes or until biscuits
are golden and filling is heated through.   *Makes 8 servings*

Note: Refrigerate leftovers up to 2 days or freeze up to 1 month. To
reheat thawed pockets, microwave about 30 seconds on HIGH or until
heated through.

Skippy Jammin' French Toast

½ cup SKIPPY® Creamy or SUPER CHUNK® Peanut Butter
8 slices white or whole wheat bread
½ cup grape, strawberry or raspberry jelly
2 eggs
½ cup milk
1 tablespoon SHEDD'S SPREAD COUNTRY CROCK® Spread

1. Evenly spread SKIPPY® Creamy Peanut Butter on 4 bread slices,
then spread jelly on remaining bread. Assemble sandwiches. Lightly dip
sandwiches in eggs beaten with milk.

2. In 12-inch nonstick skillet, melt Spread over medium heat and
lightly brown sandwiches, turning once.   *Makes 4 servings*

Prep Time: 5 minutes • **Cook Time:** 5 minutes

Apple and Cheese Pocket

Devil's Food Pancakes

1 package (about 18 ounces) devil's food cake mix
2 cups milk
2 eggs
½ cup mini chocolate chips
   Powdered sugar
   Strawberry Glaze (recipe follows, optional)

1. Whisk cake mix, milk and eggs in large bowl until well blended. Stir in chocolate chips.

2. Heat griddle or large nonstick skillet over medium-low to medium heat (350°F).* Pour ¼ cup batter onto griddle for each pancake. Cook 3 to 4 minutes or until edges appear dry; turn and cook 2 to 3 minutes. Repeat with remaining batter.

3. Sprinkle with powdered sugar and serve with Strawberry Glaze.

Makes about 22 (4-inch) pancakes

*Do not cook pancakes at a higher temperature as they burn easily.

Strawberry Glaze

1 cup chopped fresh strawberries
⅓ cup strawberry preserves

Combine strawberries and preserves in medium bowl; mix well.

Makes about 1⅓ cups glaze

Devil's Food Pancakes

Apples 'n Cinnamon Fritters

⅔ cup all-purpose flour
3 packets CREAM OF WHEAT® Apples 'n Cinnamon Instant
    Hot Cereal, uncooked
1 tablespoon sugar
1½ teaspoons baking powder
¼ teaspoon salt
⅔ cup milk
2 eggs, separated
1 tablespoon vegetable oil
    Vegetable oil for frying
    Powdered sugar (optional)

1. Mix flour, Cream of Wheat, sugar, baking powder and salt in large bowl; set aside.

2. Beat milk, egg yolks and 1 tablespoon oil with wire whisk until well blended. Add to flour mixture; stir until well blended. Let stand 10 minutes.

3. Meanwhile, heat 1½ inches oil in heavy large saucepan or electric skillet to 375°F.

4. Beat egg whites in small bowl with electric mixer on high speed until stiff peaks form. Gently stir into batter with wire whisk until well blended. Drop batter by teaspoonfuls into hot oil; cook 3 to 5 minutes or until golden brown. Remove with slotted spoon and drain on paper towels. Cool completely. Dust fritters with powdered sugar just before serving, if desired. *Makes 20 to 24 fritters*

Note: To separate eggs, pull apart the cracked egg with your thumbs. Pour the contents of the egg from one half-shell to the other, allowing the egg white to run into a bowl. Place the yolk in a separate bowl. Be sure there is no yolk in the egg whites, or they won't whip up properly.

Prep Time: 15 minutes • **Start to Finish Time:** 30 minutes

Apples 'n Cinnamon Fritters

Snack Time

Chicken Corndog Bites

1 package (11½ ounces) refrigerated corn breadstick
   dough (8 count)
1 package (10 ounces) Italian-seasoned cooked chicken
   breast strips
Mustard
Ketchup

1. Preheat oven to 375°F. Line baking sheet with parchment paper or foil.

2. Unroll dough, separate into individual breadsticks. Roll out each breadstick to 7×1½-inch rectangle (¼ inch thick). Cut each piece of dough in half crosswise to form 16 pieces total.

3. Cut chicken strips in half crosswise. Place one piece of chicken on each piece of dough; wrap dough around chicken and seal, pressing edges together tightly. Place seam side down on prepared baking sheet.

4. Bake 15 to 17 minutes or until light golden brown. Decorate with mustard and ketchup. Serve warm with additional mustard and ketchup for dipping.   *Makes 16 bites*

Pretzel Fried Eggs

24 (1-inch) pretzel rings
1 cup white chocolate chips
24 yellow candy-coated chocolate pieces

1. Line baking sheet with waxed paper. Place pretzel rings about 2 inches apart on baking sheet.

2. Place white chocolate chips in 1-quart resealable food storage bag; seal bag. Microwave on HIGH 30 seconds. Knead bag gently and microwave 30 seconds more. Repeat until chips are melted. Cut ¼-inch corner from bag.

3. Squeeze chocolate from bag onto each pretzel ring in circular motion. Fill center of pretzel first and finish with ring of chocolate around edge of pretzel. Use tip of small knife to smooth chocolate, if necessary. Place candy piece in center of each pretzel. Allow to harden at room temperature or refrigerate until set. Store in single layer in airtight container up to 1 week. *Makes 2 dozen eggs*

Variation: To make "green eggs and ham," use green candy-coated chocolate pieces for yolks. Cut small pieces of pink fruit leather for ham. Serve 2 Pretzel Fried Eggs with small strips of fruit leather bacon and square cinnamon cereal for toast.

Pretzel Fried Eggs

Parmesan Fishy Crisp

1½ sticks butter, softened
½ cup sugar
1 egg
1 cup all-purpose flour
½ cup grated Parmesan cheese
2 cups PEPPERIDGE FARM® Goldfish® Baked Snack Crackers,
  any flavor

1. Heat the oven to 350°F. Line the baking sheet with foil.

2. Beat the butter and sugar in a large mixing bowl until creamy using an electric mixer at medium speed. Beat in the egg. Gradually add flour, scraping bowl. Beat in the cheese until blended. Stir in the crackers.

3. Spread the cracker mixture in an even layer on the prepared pan. The mixture will not be in a uniform shape.

4. Bake for 20 minutes or until golden brown. (Edges may brown more quickly.) Remove from oven and let cool completely on wire rack. Break into unevenly-shaped pieces. *Makes 6 cups*

Prep Time: 15 minutes • **Bake Time:** 20 minutes

Parmesan Fishy Crisp

Bedrock Fruit Boulders

1 package (about 16 ounces) refrigerated large buttermilk biscuits
(8 biscuits)
1¼ cups finely chopped apple (about 1 small apple)
⅓ cup dried mixed fruit bits
2 tablespoons packed brown sugar
½ teaspoon ground cinnamon
1 cup sifted powdered sugar
4 to 5 teaspoons orange juice

1. Preheat oven to 350°F. Line baking sheet with parchment paper or lightly spray with nonstick cooking spray.

2. Cut each biscuit in half horizontally, making 16 rounds. Roll each round into 3½-inch circle.

3. Combine apple, dried fruit, brown sugar and cinnamon in small bowl. Spoon 1 rounded tablespoon apple mixture into center of each circle. Moisten edges of dough with water. Pull dough up and around filling, completely enclosing filling. Pinch edges to seal.

4. Place rolls, seam side down, on prepared baking sheet. Bake 16 to 18 minutes or until golden brown. Cool 10 minutes on wire rack.

5. Combine powdered sugar and enough orange juice in small bowl to make mixture of drizzling consistency. Spoon over rolls. Serve warm.

Makes 16 servings

Prep Time: 20 minutes • **Bake Time:** 16 minutes

Bedrock Fruit Boulders

Crispy Mozzarella Sticks

1 package (17.3 ounces) PEPPERIDGE FARM® Frozen Puff Pastry
   Sheets (2 sheets)
¼ cup grated Parmesan cheese
1 egg
1 tablespoon water
1 package (12 ounces) mozzarella cheese snack sticks (12 sticks)
1 cup PREGO® Marinara Italian Sauce

1. **KIDS AND ADULT:** Read the recipe, and then gather all the
ingredients and equipment needed.

2. **KIDS:** Remove the frozen pastry sheets from the package and
place on the counter to thaw for 30 minutes or until they're easy to
handle. Measure Parmesan cheese with a ¼ cup dry measuring cup
and put in a small shallow bowl.

3. **KIDS AND ADULT:** Heat the oven to 400°F. Crack the egg in a
small shallow bowl. Measure the water using 1 tablespoon measuring
spoon and add to the egg. Beat the egg and water with a fork until
they are mixed.

4. **KIDS AND ADULT:** Sprinkle some flour over a pastry cloth or large
cutting board. Unfold **1** pastry sheet on the floured surface. Cut the
pastry into 6 (5×3-inch) rectangles using a pizza wheel. Repeat with
the remaining pastry sheet.

5. **KIDS AND ADULT:** Put a mozzarella stick on the long edge of each
pastry rectangle and roll up in the pastry. Press pastry gently along
the long edge and pinch the ends to seal. Place pastry rolls seam-side
down on work surface.

6. **KIDS:** Brush the tops of sticks with the egg mixture using a pastry
brush. Dip the tops in Parmesan cheese and place cheese-side up on
ungreased baking sheet 1-inch apart. Prick the tops of the pastry rolls
with a fork 6 times down the length of each roll.

7. **ADULT:** Bake for 17 minutes or until golden. (Some cheese may
ooze out.)

continued on page 36

Crispy Mozzarella Sticks

Crispy Mozzarella Sticks, continued

8. **KIDS:** Measure Italian sauce using 1 cup liquid measuring cup and pour into a 1½-quart saucepan.

9. **ADULT:** Put the saucepan on a burner set to medium heat. Heat until warm, stirring occasionally. Pour the Italian sauce into a serving bowl.

10. **KIDS AND ADULT:** Remove the baked rolls from the baking sheet with a pancake spatula and put on a serving plate. Serve with the Italian sauce for dipping. *Makes 12 servings*

Hands-On Time: 20 minutes • **Thaw Time:** 30 minutes • **Bake Time:** 17 minutes

Happy Apple Salsa with Baked Cinnamon Pita Chips

2 teaspoons sugar
¼ teaspoon ground cinnamon
2 rounds pita bread, split
  Nonstick cooking spray
1 tablespoon jelly or jam
1 medium apple, diced
1 tablespoon finely diced celery
1 tablespoon finely diced carrot
1 tablespoon golden raisins
1 teaspoon lemon juice

1. Preheat oven to 350°F.

2. Combine sugar and cinnamon in small bowl. Cut pitas into wedges; place on ungreased baking sheet. Spray lightly with cooking spray; sprinkle with cinnamon-sugar. Bake 10 minutes or until lightly browned. Set aside to cool.

3. Meanwhile, place jelly in medium microwavable bowl; microwave on HIGH 10 seconds. Stir in apple, celery, carrot, raisins and lemon juice. Serve salsa with pita chips. *Makes 3 servings*

Happy Apple Salsa with Baked Cinnamon Pita Chips

Mysterious Colorful Jiggles

1 package (4-serving size) lime gelatin
1 package (4-serving size) orange gelatin
1 package (4-serving size) blue raspberry gelatin
   Whipped topping
   Colored sprinkles

1. Prepare lime gelatin according to package directions and place in 2-cup measuring cup or small pitcher. Pour ¼ cup lime gelatin mixture into 8 (8- to 10-ounce) clear plastic cups. Refrigerate 2 hours or until gelatin is firm.

2. Meanwhile, prepare orange gelatin according to package directions; place in 2-cup measuring cup or small pitcher. Refrigerate 1 hour or until gelatin just begins to gel.

3. Remove lime gelatin cups from refrigerator. Pour ¼ cup orange gelatin into each cup; refrigerate about 2 hours or until firm.

4. Meanwhile, prepare blue raspberry gelatin according to package directions; place in 2-cup measuring cup or small pitcher. Refrigerate 1 hour or until gelatin just begins to gel.

5. Remove gelatin cups from refrigerator. Pour ¼ cup blue raspberry gelatin into cups and refrigerate about 2 hours or until firm.

6. Serve with whipped topping and sprinkles.   *Makes 8 servings*

Mysterious Colorful Jiggles

Yam Yums

1 large (or 2 medium) sweet potatoes
¼ cup maple syrup (not pancake syrup)
2 tablespoons orange juice
2 tablespoons butter, melted
⅛ teaspoon ground nutmeg
   Salt and black pepper

1. Preheat oven to 350°F. Line baking sheet with foil.

2. Cut scrubbed, unpeeled sweet potato crosswise into ½-inch-thick slices. Place slices on cutting board; use small metal cookie cutters (1½ inch in diameter) to cut shapes and letters from slices. Or, cut out shapes with sharp knife.

3. Combine maple syrup, orange juice and butter in small bowl. Arrange potato shapes in single layer on prepared baking sheet. Season both sides with nutmeg, salt and pepper. Brush both sides generously with maple syrup mixture.

4. Bake 20 to 30 minutes or until tender, turning pieces once and basting with remaining maple mixture.   *Makes about 4 servings*

Editor's Note

Yam Yums can make learning fun! They are a wonderful tool for teaching kids how to spell their names, learn the alphabet or learn different shapes. As an added bonus, the sweet potatoes provide a healthy alternative to processed snacks.

Yam Yums

Super Salami Twists

1 egg
1 tablespoon milk
1 cup (about ¼ pound) finely chopped hard salami
2 tablespoons yellow cornmeal
1 teaspoon Italian seasoning
1 package (about 11 ounces) refrigerated breadstick dough
¾ cup pasta sauce, heated

1. Preheat oven to 375°F. Line baking sheet with foil or parchment paper.

2. Beat egg and milk in shallow dish until well blended. Combine salami, cornmeal and Italian seasoning in separate shallow dish.

3. Unroll breadstick dough. Separate into 12 pieces along perforations. Roll each piece of dough in egg mixture, then in salami mixture, gently pressing salami into dough. Twist each piece of dough twice and place on prepared baking sheet.

4. Bake 13 to 15 minutes or until golden brown. Remove to wire rack; cool 5 minutes. Serve warm with pasta sauce for dipping.

Makes 12 twists

Prep Time: 10 minutes • **Bake Time:** 13 minutes

Cherry Tomato Pops

4 mozzarella string cheese sticks (1 ounce each)
8 cherry tomatoes
3 tablespoons ranch dressing

1. Slice cheese sticks in half lengthwise. Trim stem end of each cherry tomato and remove pulp and seeds.

2. Press end of cheese stick into hollowed tomato to make cherry tomato pop. Serve with ranch dressing for dipping.   *Makes 8 pops*

Super Salami Twists

Peanut Butter-Apple Wraps

¾ cup creamy peanut butter
4 (7-inch) whole wheat or spinach tortillas
¾ cup finely chopped apple
⅓ cup shredded carrot
⅓ cup granola without raisins
1 tablespoon toasted wheat germ

1. Spread peanut butter on one side of each tortilla. Sprinkle apple, carrot, granola and wheat germ evenly over each tortilla.

2. Roll up tightly; cut in half. Serve immediately or wrap in plastic wrap and refrigerate until ready to serve.   *Makes 4 servings*

Prep Time: 5 minutes • **Chill Time:** 2 hours

Peachy Pops

1 package (16 ounces) frozen sliced peaches, softened, but not completely thawed
2 containers (6 ounces each) peach or vanilla yogurt
¼ cup honey
12 small paper cups
12 popsicle or lollipop sticks
   Colored sugar or sugar sprinkles

1. Combine peaches, yogurt and honey in food processor or blender; process about 20 seconds or until smooth.

2. Pour peach mixture into paper cups and place on baking sheet. Freeze peach mixture 1 hour or until mixture begins to harden. Push popsicle sticks into centers and freeze additional 3 hours or until firm.

3. Tear paper away from pops; roll pops in sugar. Serve immediately or return to freezer until ready to serve.   *Makes 12 servings*

Prep Time: 20 minutes • **Freeze Time:** 4 hours

Peanut Butter-Apple Wraps

Banana Roll-Ups

¼ cup creamy or crunchy almond butter
2 tablespoons mini chocolate chips
1 to 2 tablespoons milk
1 (8-inch) whole wheat flour tortilla
1 large banana, peeled

Microwave Directions

1. Combine almond butter, chocolate chips and 1 tablespoon milk in medium microwavable bowl. Microwave on MEDIUM (50%) 40 seconds; stir well. Repeat if necessary to melt chocolate. Add more milk, if necessary, to reach spreading consistency.

2. Spread almond butter mixture on tortilla. Place banana on one side of tortilla and roll up tightly. Cut into 8 slices. *Makes 2 servings*

Ham & Cheese Snacks

8 thin slices ham (about 6 ounces total)
2 tablespoons honey mustard
8 thin slices Muenster cheese (about 4 ounces total)
   Thin pretzel crisps or favorite crackers

1. Spread each ham slice with about ¾ teaspoon mustard. Top 1 slice ham with 1 slice cheese; top with second slice of ham and cheese to create two double ham and cheese stacks.

2. Starting with long side, roll up each ham and cheese stack jelly-roll style into spiral. Wrap tightly in plastic wrap; refrigerate 30 minutes or up to 24 hours.

3. Cut each ham and cheese roll into ½-inch slices. Serve on pretzel crisps. *Makes 4 servings*

Prep Time: 20 minutes • **Chill Time:** 1 hour

Banana Roll-Ups

$\mathcal{L}$unchbox

A-B-C Minestrone

1 tablespoon olive oil
1 medium onion, chopped
2 medium carrots, chopped
1 small zucchini, chopped
½ teaspoon dried Italian seasoning
4 cups chicken broth
1 jar (1 pound 10 ounces) RAGÚ® Old World Style® Pasta Sauce
1 can (15.5 ounces) cannellini or white kidney beans, rinsed and drained
1 cup alphabet pasta

1. In 4-quart saucepan, heat olive oil over medium heat and cook onion, carrots and zucchini, stirring frequently, 5 minutes or until vegetables are tender. Add Italian seasoning and cook, stirring occasionally, 1 minute. Add broth and Pasta Sauce and bring to a boil. Stir in beans and pasta. Cook, stirring occasionally, 10 minutes or until pasta is tender.

2. Serve, if desired, with chopped parsley and grated Parmesan cheese. *Makes 8 servings*

Prep Time: 10 minutes • **Cook Time:** 20 minutes

Spotted Butterfly Sandwich

2 slices raisin bread
2 tablespoons cream cheese, softened
1 teaspoon honey
⅛ teaspoon ground cinnamon
1 baby carrot
½ stalk celery
2 carrot strips
2 dried apricots

1. Stack bread slices; cut diagonally into triangles. Place on serving plate with points facing inward to form butterfly wings.

2. Combine cream cheese, honey and cinnamon in small bowl. Roll cream cheese mixture into 2 balls and place between bread slices at points, pressing down at points to lift top slice of bread.

3. Place baby carrot in center of bread slices to create body. Cut tips from celery for antennae. Decorate wings with carrot strips and apricots.   *Makes 1 sandwich*

Prep Time: 10 minutes

If your kids dislike raisins, try substituting cinnamon swirl bread for the raisin bread.

Spotted Butterfly Sandwich

Roasted Ratatouille Wraps

6 cups assorted fresh vegetables,* cut into 1-inch chunks
3 tablespoons olive oil
1 small onion, chopped
1 jar (1 pound 10 ounces) RAGÚ® Chunky Pasta Sauce
6 flour tortillas
1½ cups shredded mozzarella cheese (about 6 ounces)

Assorted fresh vegetables: use eggplant, bell pepper, yellow squash and/or zucchini.

1. Preheat oven to 400°F. Line jelly-roll pan with nonstick foil and toss vegetables with 2 tablespoons olive oil. Roast, stirring once, 35 minutes or until vegetables are tender.

2. In 12-inch nonstick skillet, heat remaining 1 tablespoon olive oil over medium heat and cook onion, stirring occasionally, 4 minutes or until tender. Add roasted vegetables and Pasta Sauce and simmer, stirring occasionally, 5 minutes or until heated through and slightly thickened.

3. Evenly spoon onto tortillas, then sprinkle with cheese. Roll.

Makes 6 servings

Prep Time: 15 minutes • **Cook Time:** 35 minutes

Bacon & Tomato Melts

4 slices crisp-cooked bacon
4 slices (1 ounce each) Cheddar cheese
1 tomato, sliced
4 slices whole wheat bread
2 tablespoons butter, melted

1. Layer 2 slices bacon, 2 slices cheese and sliced tomato on each of 2 bread slices; top with remaining bread slices. Brush sandwiches with butter.

2. Heat large grill pan or skillet over medium heat. Add sandwiches; press lightly with spatula or weigh down with small plate. Cook sandwiches 4 to 5 minutes per side or until cheese melts and sandwiches are golden brown.

Makes 2 sandwiches

Roasted Ratatouille Wraps

Hearty Pasta Fa-School Soup

1 large onion, chopped (about 1 cup)

1 medium tomato, chopped (about 1 cup)

2 cans (49 ounces each) SWANSON® Chicken Broth (about 12 cups)

1 can (about 16 ounces) white kidney (cannellini) beans, rinsed and drained

1 can (9.75 ounces) SWANSON® Premium Chunk Chicken Breast, undrained

1 cup uncooked alphabet pasta

1 tablespoon olive or vegetable oil

¼ teaspoon garlic powder

2 packages (11.25 ounces each) PEPPERIDGE FARM® Texas Toast, any variety

1. **KIDS AND ADULT:** Read the recipe, and then gather all the ingredients and equipment needed.

2. **ADULT:** Chop the onion and tomato using the knife and cutting board. Open the cans of broth, beans and chicken using the can opener.

3. **KIDS:** Measure the pasta using a 1 cup dry measuring cup. Pour the beans into a strainer over the sink. Rinse the beans with cold water and drain. Measure the oil with a 1 tablespoon measuring spoon and pour into a 6-quart saucepot.

4. **ADULT:** Put the saucepot on a burner set to medium-high heat. Add the onion and cook until the onion is tender, stirring occasionally with the wooden spoon.

5. **KIDS AND ADULT:** Pour the broth into the saucepot. Measure the garlic powder using a ¼ teaspoon measuring spoon and add to the saucepot. Increase the heat to high. Heat to a boil, stirring occasionally with a wooden spoon. Add the pasta and return the mixture to a boil, stirring occasionally. Boil for 5 minutes.

6. **KIDS AND ADULT:** Add the beans, tomato and chicken with its liquid. Reduce the heat to low. Cook for 5 minutes or until the pasta is tender.

continued on page 56

Hearty Pasta Fa-School Soup

Hearty Pasta Fa-School Soup, continued

7. **KIDS:** Remove the toast from the package and place on a baking sheet.

8. **ADULT:** Bake the toast according to the package directions.

9. **KIDS AND ADULT:** Remove the toasts from the baking sheet with a pancake spatula and put in napkin-lined serving basket. Ladle the soup into serving bowls and serve with the toasts.   *Makes 10 servings*

Hands-On Time: 15 minutes • **Cook Time:** 20 minutes

Tic-Tac-Toe Sandwich

2 teaspoons mayonnaise
1 slice whole wheat bread
1 slice white sandwich bread
1 slice cheese
1 slice deli ham
3 black or green olives

1. Spread 1 teaspoon mayonnaise on each bread slice. Layer cheese and ham on one bread slice. Top with remaining slice.

2. Trim crust from sandwich. Cut sandwich into 9 squares by cutting into thirds in each direction. Turn alternating pieces over to form checkerboard pattern.

3. Thinly slice 1 olive to form 'O's. Cut remaining 2 olives into strips. Place olive pieces on sandwich squares to form 'X's and 'O's.

Makes 1 sandwich

Prep Time: 5 minutes

Tic-Tac-Toe Sandwiches

Sloppy Joe Race Cars

1 tablespoon olive oil
1 medium onion, sliced
2 pounds ground turkey or ground beef
1 jar (1 pound 10 ounces) RAGÚ® ROBUSTO!® Pasta Sauce
¼ cup firmly packed brown sugar
2 tablespoons sweet pickle relish
8 hero rolls
   Race Car Garnishes*

*For Race Car Garnishes, use mini pretzel twists for steering wheel, zucchini or cucumber slices for wheels attached with thin pretzel or carrot sticks, radish for "driver" with black olives for eyes, carrot sticks for arms, and green pimento-stuffed olives and thinly sliced carrot rounds for headlights.

1. In 12-inch nonstick skillet, heat olive oil over medium-high heat and cook onion, stirring occasionally, 2 minutes or until tender. Add ground turkey and cook, stirring occasionally, until done.

2. Stir in Pasta Sauce, brown sugar and relish. Cover and simmer 10 minutes.

3. Meanwhile, cut out a 5×2-inch "trench" in top of rolls, removing some bread. To serve, evenly fill rolls with turkey mixture.

Makes 8 servings

Prep Time: 25 minutes • **Cook Time:** 20 minutes

Editor's Note

Use the Race Car Garnishes to introduce your kids to a variety of new food in small portions. Observe which foods they are enjoying the most, then make those foods part of other meals.

Sloppy Joe Race Car

Zippy Beef Alphabet Soup with Parmesan Toasts

1 pound ground beef (95% lean)
½ teaspoon salt
¼ teaspoon pepper
2 cups water
1 can (14 to 14½ ounces) ready-to-serve beef broth
1 can (15½ ounces) Great Northern beans, undrained
1 can (14½ ounces) Italian-style diced tomatoes, undrained
1 cup uncooked alphabet pasta
2 cups small broccoli florets
    Salt and pepper

Parmesan Toasts:
    3 slices whole wheat bread
    Olive oil for brushing
    2 tablespoons grated or shredded Parmesan cheese

1. Heat oven to 350°F. Brown ground beef in stockpot over medium heat 8 to 10 minutes or until beef is not pink, breaking up into ¾-inch crumbles. Season with ½ teaspoon salt and ¼ teaspoon pepper.

2. Add water, broth, beans, tomatoes and pasta; bring to a boil. Reduce heat; cover and simmer 5 minutes. Stir in broccoli; return to a boil. Reduce heat; cover and simmer 3 to 5 minutes or until broccoli is crisp-tender and pasta is tender. Season with salt and pepper, as desired.

3. Meanwhile prepare Parmesan Toasts. Cut out shapes from bread slices with cookie cutters. Place on baking sheet sprayed with nonstick cooking spray. Brush cutouts lightly with oil and sprinkle evenly with cheese. Bake in 350°F oven 6 to 8 minutes or until lightly toasted.

4. Serve soup with toasts; sprinkle with additional cheese, if desired.

Makes 4 servings

Prep and Cook Time: 25 to 30 minutes

Favorite recipe courtesy of **The Beef Checkoff**

Zippy Beef Alphabet Soup with Parmesan Toast

Waffled Grilled Cheese

2 tablespoons butter
2 slices bread
1 teaspoon mustard
1 slice cheese
1 slice ham

1. Preheat waffle iron. Spread 1 tablespoon butter on one side of each bread slice; spread mustard on other side. Layer cheese and ham over mustard. Top with remaining bread slice, mustard side down.

2. Spray waffle iron lightly with nonstick cooking spray. Place sandwich in waffle iron; close lid. Cook 3 to 5 minutes or until top is browned and cheese is melted. *Makes 1 serving*

Hot Dog Burritos

1 can (16 ounces) pork and beans
⅓ cup ketchup
2 tablespoons brown sugar
2 tablespoons *French's*® Classic Yellow® Mustard
8 frankfurters, cooked
8 (8-inch) flour tortillas, heated

1. Combine beans, ketchup, brown sugar and mustard in medium saucepan. Bring to boil over medium-high heat. Reduce heat to low and simmer 2 minutes.

2. Arrange frankfurters in heated tortillas and top with bean mixture. Roll up jelly-roll style. *Makes 8 servings*

Tip: Try topping dogs with **French's**® French Fried Onions before rolling up!

Prep Time: 5 minutes • **Cook Time:** 8 minutes

Waffled Grilled Cheese

Chili in Tortilla Bowls

1½ pounds ground turkey or ground beef
1 medium onion, chopped
1 large red bell pepper, diced
2 tablespoons chili powder
1 can (19 ounces) red kidney beans, rinsed and drained
1 can (11 ounces) whole kernel corn, drained
1 jar (1 pound 10 ounces) RAGÚ® Chunky Pasta Sauce
6 burrito-size whole wheat, spinach or tomato tortillas
1 cup shredded 2% Cheddar cheese (about 4 ounces)

1. In 12-inch skillet, brown ground turkey over medium-high heat, stirring occasionally. Add onion, red pepper and chili powder and cook, stirring occasionally, 5 minutes or until onion is tender. Stir in beans, corn and Pasta Sauce.

2. Bring to a boil over high heat. Reduce heat to low and simmer, covered, stirring occasionally, 20 minutes.

3. Meanwhile, using one tortilla at a time, press into a 1- or 2-cup microwave-safe bowl to form bowl shape. Microwave at HIGH 1½ minutes. Let cool 1 minute. Gently lift out and arrange on serving plate. Repeat with remaining tortillas.

4. To serve, spoon chili into tortilla bowls, then sprinkle with cheese.

Makes 6 servings

Prep Time: 10 minutes • **Cook Time:** 25 minutes

Chili in Tortilla Bowl

Turkey Bacon Mini Wafflewiches

1 teaspoon Dijon mustard
1 teaspoon honey
8 frozen mini waffles (2 pieces, divided into individual waffles)
2 thin slices deli turkey, cut into thin strips
2 tablespoons cooked and crumbled bacon
4 teaspoons shredded Cheddar or mozzarella cheese
2 teaspoons butter

1. Combine mustard and honey in small bowl. Spread small amount of mustard mixture onto one side of 4 waffles. Top each with turkey strips and bacon; sprinkle with cheese. Top with 4 remaining waffles.

2. Melt butter in medium nonstick skillet over medium heat. Pressing with back of spatula, cook sandwiches 3 to 4 minutes per side or until cheese melts and waffles are golden brown.   *Makes 2 servings*

Funny Face Sandwich Melts

2 super-size English muffins, split and toasted
8 teaspoons *French's®* Honey Mustard
1 can (8 ounces) crushed pineapple, drained
8 ounces sliced smoked ham
4 slices Swiss cheese or white American cheese

1. Place English muffins, cut side up, on baking sheet. Spread each with *2 teaspoons* mustard. Arrange one-fourth of the pineapple, ham and cheese on top, dividing evenly.

2. Broil until cheese melts, about 1 minute. Decorate with mustard and assorted vegetables to create your own funny face.

Makes 4 servings

Prep Time: 10 minutes • **Cook Time:** 1 minute

Turkey Bacon Mini Wafflewiches

Calzone-on-a-Stick

8 wooden craft sticks
8 turkey or chicken sausage links (about 1½ pounds), cooked
1 package (16.3 ounces) refrigerated grand-size biscuits
1 jar (1 pound 10 ounces) RAGÚ® Old World Style® Pasta Sauce
4 mozzarella cheese sticks, halved lengthwise

1. Preheat oven to 350°F. Insert craft stick halfway into each sausage; set aside.

2. Separate biscuits. On lightly floured surface, roll each biscuit into 7×4-inch oval. Place 2 tablespoons Pasta Sauce on long side of each oval. Top with sausage and ½ mozzarella stick. Fold dough over and pinch edges to seal. On greased baking sheet, arrange calzones seam-side down.

3. Bake 15 minutes or until golden. Serve with remaining Pasta Sauce, heated, for dipping.   *Makes 8 servings*

Prep Time: 20 minutes • **Cook Time:** 15 minutes

Bagel Dogs with Spicy Red Sauce

1 cup ketchup
1 medium onion, finely chopped
¼ cup packed brown sugar
1 tablespoon cider vinegar
2 teaspoons hot pepper sauce
1 clove garlic, minced
1 teaspoon Worcestershire sauce
1 teaspoon liquid smoke
4 bagel dogs

1. Combine all ingredients except bagel dogs in medium saucepan. Heat mixture over medium-high heat until boiling. Reduce heat; simmer 5 minutes, stirring occasionally.

2. Prepare bagel dogs according to package directions. Serve with sauce.   *Makes 4 servings*

Calzone-on-a-Stick

Party Favorites

Birthday Cake Cookies

1 package (about 18 ounces) refrigerated sugar cookie dough
1 container (16 ounces) prepared white frosting
  Food coloring (optional)
  Colored sprinkles or decors
10 small birthday candles

1. Preheat oven to 350°F. Lightly grease 10 mini (1¾-inch) muffin cups and 10 standard (2½-inch) muffin cups. Shape one third of dough into 10 (1-inch) balls; press onto bottoms and up sides of prepared mini muffin cups. Shape remaining two thirds of dough into 10 equal balls; press onto bottoms and up sides of prepared standard muffin cups.

2. Bake mini cookies 8 to 9 minutes or until edges are light brown. Bake standard-size cookies 10 to 11 minutes or until edges are light brown. Cool 5 minutes in pans on wire racks. Remove cookies to wire racks; cool completely.

3. Add food coloring, if desired, to frosting; mix well. Spread frosting over top and side of each cookie. Place 1 mini cookie on top of 1 regular cookie. Decorate with sprinkles. Press 1 candle into center of each cookie cake. *Makes 10 cookie cakes*

Christmas Tree Treats

¾ cup (1½ sticks) plus 2 tablespoons butter, softened
½ cup sugar
½ teaspoon almond extract
1¾ cups all-purpose flour
½ teaspoon baking powder
¼ teaspoon salt
   Green food coloring
18 flat wooden popsicle sticks (at least 5 inches long)
   Prepared icings and decors (optional)

1. Beat butter and sugar in large bowl with electric mixer at medium speed until well blended. Add almond extract; beat until blended. Combine flour, baking powder and salt in small bowl; gradually add to butter mixture, beating after each addition. Add food coloring until desired shade of green is reached. Divide dough in half; shape halves into 1-inch logs. Wrap in plastic wrap; refrigerate 2 hours.

2. Preheat oven to 275°F. Lightly grease cookie sheets or line with parchment paper. Place wooden sticks on prepared cookie sheets. Cut dough into ½-inch-thick slices. For each tree, place 3 slices next to each other half way up from bottom of stick; place 2 slices above them, overlapping bottom slices slightly. Place 1 slice at top of tree, overlapping middle slices slightly.

3. Bake about 30 minutes or until edges are lightly browned. Cool on cookie sheets 5 minutes; remove to wire racks to cool completely. Decorate with icings and decors, if desired.

Makes 1½ dozen large cookies

Christmas Tree Treats

Pretty Princess Cake

1 package (about 18 ounces) cake mix (any flavor), plus
    ingredients to prepare mix
1 (8-inch) washable doll or doll cake pick
    Fruit leather, any flavor
8 to 10 large marshmallows
1 container (16 ounces) white frosting
    Food coloring (any color)
    Assorted candies

1. Prepare and bake cake according to package directions for 12-cup bundt cake. Cool completely before frosting.

2. Wrap doll torso and body with fruit leather to resemble clothing.

3. Place cake on serving plate. Place about 4 marshmallows in center of cake. Press doll into marshmallows; continue adding marshmallows around doll until center is filled and doll is stable and at desired height.

4. Blend frosting and food coloring in medium bowl until desired shade is reached. Frost cake, swirling frosting with spatula or knife. Decorate cake with assorted candies.   *Makes 12 servings*

Editor's Note

Celebrate a girl's next birthday with one of our most charming cakes. You can customize it to her liking by making her favorite kind of cake mix and decorating it with her favorite colors and candies. It will be a special memory for years to come.

Pretty Princess Cake

Fluffy Cottontails

¾ cup sugar
½ cup (1 stick) unsalted butter, softened
½ cup shortening
1 teaspoon vanilla
2 cups all-purpose flour
⅔ cup malted milk powder
¼ teaspoon salt
　Malted milk balls
　Assorted colored decorating icings
　Mini marshmallows

1. Preheat oven to 350°F. Lightly grease cookie sheets. Beat sugar, butter, shortening and vanilla in large bowl. Add flour, malted milk powder and salt until well blended.

2. For bunny bodies, shape heaping teaspoonfuls of dough around malted milk balls. For bunny heads, shape scant teaspoonfuls of dough into balls. For each bunny, press body and head together on prepared cookie sheets. Shape ½ teaspoon of dough into 2 ears; press gently into head.

3. Bake 8 minutes or until lightly browned. Let cookies cool 1 minute on cookie sheets. Remove to wire racks; cool completely.

4. Decorate cookies with icings as desired. Cut marshmallows in half; immediately place marshmallow halves on cookies to resemble bunny tails. Let cookies stand until icing is set.　　*Makes 2½ dozen cookies*

Fluffy Cottontails

Yummy Mummy Cookies

⅔ cup butter or margarine, softened
1 cup sugar
2 teaspoons vanilla extract
2 eggs
2½ cups all-purpose flour
½ cup HERSHEY₀S Cocoa
½ teaspoon salt
¼ teaspoon baking soda
1 cup HERSHEY₀S Mini Chips Semi-Sweet Chocolate
1 to 2 packages (12 ounces each) HERSHEY₀S Premier White Chips
1 to 2 tablespoons shortening (do *not* use butter, margarine, spread or oil)
Additional HERSHEY₀S Mini Chips Semi-Sweet Chocolate

1. Beat butter, sugar and vanilla in large bowl until creamy. Add eggs; beat well. Stir together flour, cocoa, salt and baking soda; gradually add to butter mixture, beating until blended. Stir in 1 cup small chocolate chips. Refrigerate dough 15 to 20 minutes or until firm enough to handle.

2. Heat oven to 350°F. To form body, using 1 tablespoon dough, roll into 3½-inch carrot shape; place on ungreased cookie sheet. To form head, using 1 teaspoon dough, roll into ball the size and shape of a grape; press onto wide end of body. Repeat with remaining dough.

3. Bake 8 to 9 minutes or until set. Cool slightly; remove from cookie sheet to wire rack. Cool completely. Place 2 cups (12-ounce package) white chips and 1 tablespoon shortening in microwave-safe shallow bowl. Microwave at MEDIUM (50%) 1 minute; stir until melted.

4. Coat tops of cookies by placing one cookie at a time on table knife or narrow metal spatula; spoon white chip mixture evenly over cookie to coat. (If mixture begins to thicken, return to microwave for a few seconds). Place coated cookies on wax paper. Melt additional chips with shortening, if needed, for additional coating. As coating begins to set on cookies, using a toothpick, score lines and facial features into coating to resemble mummy. Place 2 small chocolate chips on each cookie for eyes. Store, covered, in cool, dry place.

Makes about 30 cookies

Yummy Mummy Cookies

Fun Fort

1 package (about 18 ounces) devil's food cake mix, plus
   ingredients to prepare mix
1 container (16 ounces) chocolate fudge frosting
6 square chocolate-covered snack cakes
9 cream-filled wafer cookies
1 tube (4¼ ounces) chocolate decorating icing
1 tube (4¼ ounces) white decorating icing
1 tube (4¼ ounces) green decorating icing with tips
   Sprinkles
   Paper flag and plastic figurines (optional)

1. Prepare and bake cake mix in two 8-inch square baking pans according to package directions. Cool in pans on wire racks 15 minutes. Remove from pans; cool completely.

2. Place 1 cake layer upside down on serving platter; frost top. Place second layer upside down on first cake layer so cake top is completely flat. Frost top and sides. Place one square snack cake in each corner of large cake. Cut remaining two snack cakes in half diagonally; place 1 half cut side down on each snack cake in corners.

3. Attach wafer cookies with chocolate icing to cake for fence posts, front gate and flagpole. Decorate fort with chocolate, white and green icings and sprinkles as desired. Attach flag to flagpole with chocolate icing and place figurines on top of cake, if desired.

Makes 12 servings

Kitchen Tip

If two or more baking pans are used, allow at least an inch of space between the pans. Plus two inches between the pans and the walls of the oven for proper heat circulation.

Fun Fort

Gobbler Cookies

1 package (about 18 ounces) refrigerated sugar cookie dough
¼ cup all-purpose flour
2 teaspoons ground cinnamon
   Red, yellow, orange and white decorating icings
   Chocolate sprinkles, mini chocolate chips and red licorice

1. Preheat oven to 350°F. Lightly grease cookie sheets. Remove dough from wrapper; place in large bowl. Let dough stand at room temperature about 15 minutes.

2. Add flour and cinnamon to dough; beat with electric mixer at medium speed until well blended.

3. Shape dough into 12 large (1½-inch) balls, 12 medium (1-inch) balls and 12 small (¾-inch) balls.

4. Flatten large balls into 4-inch rounds on prepared cookie sheets; freeze 10 minutes. Bake 9 to 11 minutes or until lightly browned. Remove to wire racks; cool completely.

5. Flatten medium balls into 2¼-inch rounds on prepared cookie sheets; freeze 10 minutes. Bake 8 to 10 minutes or until lightly browned. Remove to wire racks; cool completely.

6. Flatten small balls into 1-inch rounds on prepared cookie sheets; freeze 10 minutes. Bake 6 to 8 minutes or until lightly browned. Remove to wire racks; cool completely.

7. Decorate large cookies with red, yellow and orange icings and chocolate sprinkles to make feathers. Place medium cookies on large cookies, towards bottom; place small cookies above medium cookies. Decorate turkeys as shown in photo using icings, chocolate chips and licorice to make eyes, beaks, gobblers and feet. Let stand 20 minutes or until set. *Makes 1 dozen large cookies*

Gobbler Cookies

St. Pat's Pudding Pies

1 package (4-serving size) pistachio pudding and pie filling mix
  plus ingredients to prepare mix
1 package mini graham cracker pie crusts (6 crusts)
  Assorted candies and colored sprinkles
  Green gumdrops

1. Prepare pudding according to package directions. Divide pudding evenly among crusts. Decorate with candies and sprinkles as desired.

2. For gumdrop shamrocks, roll gumdrops on heavily sugared surface until fairly flat. Cut into shamrock shapes with small cookie cutter. Place in centers of pies. Refrigerate leftovers. *Makes 6 servings*

Surprise Package Cupcakes

1 package (about 18 ounces) cake mix, any flavor, plus
  ingredients to prepare mix
  Food coloring
1 container (16 ounces) vanilla frosting
1 tube (4¼ ounces) white decorating icing
72 chewy fruit squares
  Colored decors

1. Preheat oven to 350°F. Line 24 standard (2½-inch) muffin cups with paper baking cups or spray with nonstick cooking spray.

2. Prepare cake mix and bake in prepared muffin cups according to package directions. Cool cupcakes in pans on wire racks 15 minutes. Remove to racks; cool completely.

3. Stir food coloring into frosting in small bowl until desired shade is reached. Frost cupcakes.

4. Use icing to pipe ribbons on fruit squares to resemble wrapped presents. Place 3 candy presents on each cupcake. Decorate with decors. *Makes 24 cupcakes*

St. Pat's Pudding Pies

Uncle Sam's Hat

1 package (about 18 ounces) refrigerated chocolate chip
    cookie dough
2 cups powdered sugar
2 to 4 tablespoons milk
    Red and blue food colorings

1. Preheat oven to 350°F. Lightly grease 12-inch round pizza pan and cookie sheet. Remove dough from wrapper. Press dough evenly into prepared pizza pan; cut into hat shape as shown in photo. Press scraps together and flatten heaping tablespoons of dough on prepared cookie sheet. Using 1½- to 2-inch star cookie cutter, cut out 3 stars; remove and discard dough scraps.

2. Bake stars 5 to 7 minutes and hat 7 to 9 minutes or until lightly browned at edges. Cool stars on cookie sheet 1 minute. Remove stars to wire rack; cool completely. Cool hat completely in pan on rack.

3. Combine powdered sugar and enough milk, 1 tablespoon at a time, to make medium-thick pourable glaze. Spread small amount of glaze over stars and place on waxed paper; let stand until glaze is set. Using red and blue food colorings, tint ½ of glaze red, tint ¼ of glaze blue and leave remaining ¼ of glaze white.

4. Decorate hat with red, white and blue glazes as shown in photo; arrange stars on blue band of hat. Let stand until glaze is set.

Makes 1 large cookie

Kitchen Tip

Food colorings are edible dyes, usually red, green, blue and yellow, used to tint frostings and candies. The most popular are liquid colors available at supermarkets. When stored tightly closed in a cool, dry place, liquid colors will last four years.

Uncle Sam's Hat

Happy Clown Face

1 package (about 18 ounces) white cake mix, plus ingredients to prepare mix
1 container (16 ounces) white frosting
Food coloring (any color)
Assorted gumdrops, gummy candies, colored licorice strings and other candies
1 party hat
Candles

1. Prepare and bake cake mix according to package directions for two 8- or 9-inch round cake layers. Cool completely before frosting.

2. Combine frosting and food coloring in medium bowl until desired shade is reached. Place one cake layer on serving plate; spread with frosting. Top with second cake layer; frost top and side of cake.

3. Decorate face of clown using assorted candies. Arrange party hat and candles on cake as desired. *Makes 12 servings*

Conversation Heart Cereal Treats

20 large marshmallows
2 tablespoons butter or margarine
3 cups frosted oat cereal with marshmallow bits
12 large conversation hearts

1. Line 8- or 9-inch square pan with foil, leaving 2-inch overhang on 2 sides. Generously grease or spray with nonstick cooking spray.

2. Melt marshmallows and butter in medium saucepan over medium heat 3 minutes or until melted and smooth, stirring constantly. Remove from heat.

3. Add cereal; stir until completely coated. Spread in prepared pan; press evenly onto bottom using greased rubber spatula. Press heart candies into top of treats while still warm, evenly spacing to allow 1 heart per bar. Let cool 10 minutes. Remove treats from pan using foil as handles. Cut into bars. *Makes 12 bars*

Happy Clown Face

Giant Gift Boxes

1 package (about 18 ounces) chocolate or vanilla cake mix, plus
    ingredients to prepare mix
1 container (16 ounces) white frosting
    Green and orange food coloring
    Yellow decorating icing
    Candy sprinkles

1. Prepare and bake cake mix according to package directions for two 8- or 9-inch square cakes. Cool completely before frosting.

2. Blend half of frosting and green food coloring in medium bowl until desired shade is reached. Repeat with remaining frosting and orange food coloring.

3. Place one cake layer on serving plate; frost top and sides with green frosting. Pipe stripe of icing on each side to resemble ribbon. Let frosting set before adding second cake layer. Place second cake layer slightly off-center and rotated 45 degrees from bottom layer as shown in photo. Frost top and sides with orange frosting. Pipe stripe of icing on each side to resemble ribbon.

4. Pipe additional icing on top of cake for bow and streamers as shown in photo. Decorate cake with candy sprinkles, if desired.

Makes 12 servings

Giant Gift Boxes

Dinner Fun

Polka Dot Lasagna Skillet

1 pound ground beef or turkey
1 package lasagna and sauce meal kit
4 cups hot water
½ cup ricotta cheese
1 egg
3 tablespoons grated Parmesan cheese
2 tablespoons all-purpose flour
2 tablespoons chopped fresh parsley
½ teaspoon Italian seasoning
¼ teaspoon black pepper

1. Brown beef 6 to 8 minutes in large skillet over medium-high heat, stirring to break up meat. Drain fat.

2. Stir in contents of meal kit and hot water; bring to a boil. Reduce heat to low; cover and cook 10 minutes.

3. Meanwhile, blend ricotta, egg, Parmesan, flour, parsley, Italian seasoning and pepper in small bowl until smooth. Drop tablespoonfuls of ricotta mixture over pasta; cover and cook 4 to 5 minutes or until dumplings are set. Remove from heat; let stand about 4 minutes before serving. *Makes 4 to 6 servings*

Mom's Tuna Casserole

2 cans (12 ounces each) tuna, drained and flaked
3 cups diced celery
3 cups crushed potato chips, divided
6 hard-cooked eggs, chopped
1 can (10¾ ounces) condensed cream of mushroom soup,
    undiluted
1 can (10¾ ounces) condensed cream of celery soup, undiluted
1 cup mayonnaise
1 teaspoon dried tarragon
1 teaspoon black pepper

Slow Cooker Directions

1. Combine tuna, celery, 2½ cups potato chips, eggs, soups, mayonnaise, tarragon and pepper in slow cooker; stir well.

2. Cover; cook on LOW 5 to 8 hours.

3. Sprinkle with remaining ½ cup potato chips.   *Makes 8 servings*

Oven-Baked Chicken Parmesan

4 boneless, skinless chicken breast halves (about 1¼ pounds)
1 egg, lightly beaten
¾ cup Italian seasoned dry bread crumbs
1 jar (1 pound 10 ounces) RAGÚ® Old World Style® Pasta Sauce
1 cup shredded mozzarella cheese (about 4 ounces)

1. Preheat oven to 400°F. Dip chicken in egg, then bread crumbs, coating well.

2. In 13×9-inch glass baking dish, arrange chicken. Bake uncovered 20 minutes.

3. Pour Ragú Pasta Sauce over chicken, then top with cheese. Bake an additional 10 minutes or until chicken is thoroughly cooked. Serve, if desired, with hot cooked pasta.   *Makes 4 servings*

Prep Time: 10 minutes • **Cook Time:** 30 minutes

Mom's Tuna Casserole

Cheesy Stuffed Meatballs & Spaghetti

1 pound ground beef
½ cup Italian seasoned dry bread crumbs
1 egg
2 ounces mozzarella cheese, cut into 12 (½-inch) cubes
1 jar (1 pound 10 ounces) RAGÚ® Old World Style® Pasta Sauce
8 ounces spaghetti, cooked and drained

1. In medium bowl, combine ground beef, bread crumbs and egg; shape into 12 meatballs. Press 1 cheese cube into each meatball, enclosing completely.

2. In 3-quart saucepan, bring Pasta Sauce to a boil over medium-high heat. Gently stir in uncooked meatballs.

3. Reduce heat to low and simmer, covered, stirring occasionally, 20 minutes or until meatballs are done. Serve over hot spaghetti. Sprinkle, if desired, with grated Parmesan cheese.

Makes 4 servings

Prep Time: 20 minutes • **Cook Time:** 20 minutes

Dizzy Dogs

12 hot dogs
1 package (about 11 ounces) refrigerated breadstick dough (12 breadsticks)
1 egg white
Sesame seeds and poppy seeds
Mustard, ketchup and barbecue sauce (optional)

1. Preheat oven to 375°F.

2. Wrap each hot dog with 1 piece dough in spiral pattern. Brush with egg white and sprinkle with sesame seeds and poppy seeds. Place on ungreased baking sheet.

3. Bake 12 to 15 minutes or until light golden brown. Serve with condiments for dipping, if desired.

Makes 12 servings

Cheesy Stuffed Meatballs & Spaghetti

Octo-Dogs and Shells

4 hot dogs
1½ cups uncooked small shell pasta
1½ cups frozen mixed vegetables
1 cup prepared Alfredo sauce
Yellow mustard in squeeze bottle
Cheese-flavored fish-shaped crackers

1. Lay 1 hot dog on cutting surface. Starting 1 inch from one end of hot dog, slice hot dog vertically in half. Roll hot dog ¼ turn. Starting 1 inch from same end, slice in half vertically again, making 4 segments connected at top. Slice each segment in half vertically, creating a total of 8 "legs." Repeat with remaining hot dogs.

2. Place hot dogs in medium saucepan; cover with water. Bring to a boil over medium-high heat. Remove from heat; set aside.

3. Prepare pasta according to package directions, stirring in vegetables during last 3 minutes of cooking time. Drain; return to pan. Stir in Alfredo sauce. Heat over low heat until heated through. Divide pasta mixture between 4 plates.

4. Drain octo-dogs. Arrange one octo-dog on top of pasta mixture on each plate. Draw faces on "heads" of octo-dogs with mustard. Sprinkle crackers over pasta.   *Makes 4 servings*

Editor's Note

Octo-dogs add a fun new twist to ordinary hot dogs. Kids love these silly creatures, and with no special ingredients or equipment required, parents love them too!

Octo-Dog and Shells

Happy-Face Kids' Pizza

1¼ cups all-purpose flour
⅔ cup CREAM OF WHEAT® Hot Cereal (Instant, 1-minute,
    2½-minute or 10-minute cook time), uncooked
1 teaspoon baking powder
½ cup milk
¼ cup olive oil
1 cup pizza or tomato sauce
1 cup shredded mozzarella cheese
    Optional toppings: sliced pepperoni, sliced green olives, sliced
    black olives, red bell pepper slices

1. Preheat oven to 450°F. Spray baking pan with nonstick cooking spray.

2. Place flour, Cream of Wheat and baking powder in food processor; pulse several times. Combine milk and oil in measuring cup. While food processor is running, pour in milk mixture. Pulse several times until dough forms a ball. (If dough doesn't come together, add more flour, 1 teaspoon at a time.)

3. Turn dough onto lightly floured surface. Gently knead 5 to 6 times. Divide into 4 pieces. Roll each piece into round shape. Place dough pieces on prepared pan.

4. Spread sauce over pizzas and sprinkle cheese evenly over pizzas. Arrange pepperoni, olives and bell pepper slices to make faces, as desired. Bake 15 to 20 minutes.   *Makes 4 servings*

Variation: For Greek salad pizza, top the pizzas with a sprinkle of dried oregano, sliced olives and sliced red onions before baking, then top with shredded lettuce, chopped tomatoes and crumbled feta cheese. Or use your favorite toppings to make a variety of pizzas for kids and adults alike.

Prep Time: 10 minutes • **Start to Finish Time:** 30 minutes

Happy-Face Kids' Pizza

Mini Pickle Sea Monster Burgers

4 large hamburger buns
2 whole dill pickles
1 pound ground beef
2 tablespoons steak sauce
 Salt and black pepper
3 American cheese slices, cut into 4 squares each
 Ketchup

1. Preheat broiler. Spray broiler rack and pan with nonstick cooking spray; set aside.

2. Cut 3 circles out of each bun half with 2-inch biscuit cutter; set aside. Discard scraps (or reserve to make bread crumbs for another use).*

3. Slice pickles lengthwise into thin slices. Using 12 largest slices, cut 4 to 5 slits on one end of each slice, about ½ inch deep; fan slightly to resemble fish tails. Set aside. Save remaining slices for another use.

4. Combine ground beef and steak sauce in medium bowl; mix until just blended. Shape meat into 12 (2½×¼-inch) patties. Place on broiler rack. Sprinkle with salt and pepper. Broil 4 inches from heat 2 minutes. Turn patties and broil 2 minutes longer or until no longer pink in center. Remove from heat; top with cheese squares.

5. Arrange bun bottoms on serving platter; top with ketchup and pickle slices, making sure slices stick out at both ends. Place cheeseburgers on top of pickles; top with bun tops. Place drop of ketchup on uncut end of pickle to resemble eye.

Makes 12 mini burgers

To make bread crumbs from scraps, bake on a baking sheet in a 325°F oven until very dry and lightly browned. Place the cooled, toasted bread in a resealable food storage bag and seal. Roll with a rolling pin until fine crumbs form.

Mini Pickle Sea Monster Burgers

Zippity Hot Doggity Tacos

1 small onion, finely chopped
1 tablespoon *Frank's® RedHot®* Original Cayenne Pepper Sauce
   or *French's®* Worcestershire Sauce
4 frankfurters, chopped
1 can (10½ ounces) red kidney or black beans, drained
1 can (8 ounces) tomato sauce
1 teaspoon chili powder
8 taco shells, heated
1 cup *French's®* French Fried Onions
   Garnish: chopped tomatoes, shredded lettuce, sliced olives,
   sour cream, shredded cheese

1. Heat *1 tablespoon oil* in 12-inch nonstick skillet over medium-high heat. Cook onion 3 minutes or until crisp-tender. Stir in remaining ingredients. Bring to boiling. Reduce heat to medium-low and cook 5 minutes, stirring occasionally.

2. To serve, spoon chili into taco shells. Garnish as desired and sprinkle with French Fried Onions. Splash on **Frank's RedHot** Sauce for extra zip!   *Makes 4 servings*

Prep Time: 5 minutes • **Cook Time:** 8 minutes

Kitchen Tip

To heat the taco shells in the microwave, place them on a paper towel. Heat at HIGH 20 to 30 seconds or just until warm. If you want to heat only 1 or 2 taco shells, reduce the cooking time to 10 to 15 seconds.

Zippity Hot Doggity Tacos

Stuffed Corn Bread

1¼ cups all-purpose flour
¾ cup yellow cornmeal
2 tablespoons sugar
2 teaspoons baking powder
½ teaspoon salt
1 cup milk
¼ cup vegetable oil
1 egg
½ cup (2 ounces) diced Cheddar cheese, divided
2 thin slices deli ham, diced
¼ cup tomato or pasta sauce

1. Preheat oven to 350°F. Spray 3 mini (5×3-inch) loaf pans with nonstick cooking spray.

2. Combine flour, cornmeal, sugar, baking powder and salt in medium bowl. Whisk milk, oil and egg in small bowl. Pour milk mixture over flour mixture; stir just until moistened.

3. Spoon half of batter evenly into prepared pans. Layer half of cheese, ham and tomato sauce over batter; top with remaining batter and cheese.

4. Bake about 30 minutes or until edges are browned and toothpick inserted into centers comes out clean. Cool in pans on wire racks 5 minutes. Remove from pans; slice and serve warm.

Makes 6 servings

Prep Time: 20 minutes • **Bake Time:** 30 minutes

Stuffed Corn Bread

Little Piggy Pies

2 cups frozen mixed vegetables (carrots, potatoes, peas, celery, green beans, corn, onions and/or lima beans)
1 can (10¾ ounces) condensed cream of chicken soup, undiluted
8 ounces chopped cooked chicken
⅓ cup plain yogurt
⅓ cup water
½ teaspoon dried thyme
¼ teaspoon poultry seasoning or ground sage
⅛ teaspoon garlic powder
1 package (10 biscuits) refrigerated buttermilk biscuits

1. Preheat oven to 400°F.

2. Remove 10 green peas from frozen mixed vegetables. Combine remaining vegetables, soup, chicken, yogurt, water, thyme, poultry seasoning and garlic powder in medium saucepan. Bring to a boil, stirring frequently. Cover; keep warm.

3. Press 5 biscuits into 3-inch circles. Cut remaining biscuits into 8 wedges. Place 2 wedges on top of each circle; fold points down to form ears. Roll 1 wedge into small ball; place in center of each circle to form pig's snout. Use tip of spoon handle to make indents in snout for nostrils. Place 2 reserved green peas on each circle for eyes.

4. Spoon hot chicken mixture into 5 (10-ounce) custard cups. Place a biscuit "pig" on top of each. Place remaining biscuit wedges around each "pig" on top of chicken mixture, twisting one wedge "tail" for each. Bake 9 to 11 minutes or until biscuits are golden brown.

Makes 5 servings

Prep Time: 10 minutes • **Bake Time:** 11 minutes

Little Piggy Pie

Pizza Pinwheels

2 packages (13.8 ounces each) refrigerated pizza crust dough
1 jar (1 pound 10 ounces) RAGÚ® Robusto!® Pasta Sauce
1 cup shredded mozzarella cheese (about 4 ounces)
1 cup sliced pepperoni, chopped (about 4 ounces)

1. Preheat oven to 425°F. With rolling pin or hands, press each pizza crust dough into 12×8-inch rectangle, then cut each into 4 equal squares.

2. On two greased baking sheets, arrange squares. With knife, starting at corner of each square, cut toward center of square, stopping ½ inch from center. Evenly top each square with 2 tablespoons Pasta Sauce, then cheese and pepperoni. Fold every other point into center; press to seal. Bake 10 minutes or until crusts are golden. Serve with remaining Sauce, heated.   *Makes 8 pinwheels*

Prep Time: 15 minutes • **Cook Time:** 10 minutes

Golden Chicken Nuggets

1 pound boneless skinless chicken, cut into 1½-inch pieces
¼ cup *French's*® Honey Mustard
2 cups *French's*® French Fried Onions, finely crushed

1. Preheat oven to 400°F. Toss chicken with mustard in medium bowl.

2. Place French Fried Onions into resealable plastic food storage bag. Toss chicken in onions, a few pieces at a time, pressing gently to adhere.

3. Place nuggets in shallow baking pan. Bake 15 minutes or until chicken is no longer pink in center. Serve with additional honey mustard.   *Makes 4 servings*

Prep Time: 5 minutes • **Cook Time:** 15 minutes

Pizza Pinwheel

Cheesy Potato Head

4 small baking potatoes
⅓ cup sour cream
¼ teaspoon salt
⅛ teaspoon garlic powder
⅛ teaspoon black pepper
½ cup (2 ounces) shredded Cheddar cheese, plus additional for decorating
¼ cup finely chopped broccoli (optional)
16 slices pimiento-stuffed olives
4 small broccoli florets
4 small pieces red bell pepper
4 pretzel twists

1. Preheat oven to 425°F. Pierce potatoes several times with fork; place on 15×10-inch jelly-roll pan. Bake 55 to 65 minutes or until tender. Let stand 10 minutes.

2. Cut thin slice lengthwise from one side of each potato; discard. Scoop pulp from potatoes into medium bowl, leaving ¼-inch shell.

3. Mash potato pulp with potato masher. Stir in sour cream, salt, garlic powder and black pepper. Fold in cheese and broccoli, if desired. Spoon potato mixture into shells; return to jelly-roll pan. Bake, uncovered, 20 to 25 minutes or until heated through.

4. Make face on each potato using olive slices for eyes and ears, broccoli floret for nose, cheese for hair and bell pepper for mouth.

5. Break bottom off each pretzel twist; set aside. Press pretzel tops into each potato, encircling the eyes like eyeglasses. Place reserved pretzel bottoms around olive ears to resemble eyeglass arms.

Makes 4 servings

Prep Time: 20 minutes • **Bake Time:** 75 to 90 minutes

Cheesy Potato Head

Sweet Endings

Frozen Chocolate-Covered Bananas

2 ripe medium bananas
4 wooden sticks
½ cup granola cereal without raisins
⅓ cup hot fudge topping, at room temperature

1. Line baking sheet with waxed paper; set aside.

2. Peel bananas; cut each in half crosswise. Insert wooden stick into center of cut end of each banana about 1½ inches into banana half. Place on prepared baking sheet; freeze until firm, at least 2 hours.

3. Place granola in large resealable food storage bag; crush slightly using rolling pin or meat mallet. Transfer granola to shallow plate. Place hot fudge topping in shallow dish.

4. Working with 1 banana at a time, place frozen banana in hot fudge topping; turn banana and spread topping evenly onto banana with spatula. Immediately place banana on plate with granola; turn to coat. Return to baking sheet in freezer. Repeat with remaining bananas.

5. Freeze until hot fudge topping is very firm, at least 2 hours. Place on small plates; let stand 5 minutes before serving. *Makes 4 servings*

Dessert Nachos

3 (6- to 7-inch) flour tortillas
Nonstick cooking spray
1 tablespoon sugar
⅛ teaspoon ground cinnamon
Dash ground allspice
1 container (6 to 8 ounces) vanilla yogurt
1 teaspoon grated orange peel
1½ cups strawberries
½ cup blueberries
4 teaspoons mini semisweet chocolate chips

1. Preheat oven to 375°F.

2. Cut each tortilla into 8 wedges. Place on ungreased baking sheet. Generously spray tortilla wedges with cooking spray. Combine sugar, cinnamon and allspice in small bowl. Sprinkle over tortilla wedges. Bake 7 to 9 minutes or until lightly browned; cool completely.

3. Meanwhile, combine yogurt and orange peel. Stem strawberries; cut lengthwise into quarters.

4. Place 6 tortilla wedges on each of 4 small plates. Top with strawberries and blueberries. Drizzle with yogurt mixture on top. Sprinkle with chocolate chips. Serve immediately.

Makes 4 servings

Editor's Note

What a tasty way to turn your kid into a berry lover! Strawberries and blueberries combine with yogurt and chocolate chips to put a sweet and healthy spin on everyone's favorite Mexican dish.

Dessert Nachos

Peanut Butter Chips and Jelly Bars

1½ cups all-purpose flour
½ cup sugar
¾ teaspoon baking powder
½ cup (1 stick) cold butter or margarine
1 egg, beaten
¾ cup grape jelly
1⅔ cups (10-ounce package) REESE'S® Peanut Butter Chips,
   divided

1. Heat oven to 375°F. Grease 9-inch square baking pan.

2. Stir together flour, sugar and baking powder in large bowl. Cut in butter with pastry blender or two knives until mixture resembles coarse crumbs. Add egg; blend well. Reserve 1 cup mixture; press remaining mixture onto bottom of prepared pan. Stir jelly to soften; spread evenly over crust. Sprinkle 1 cup peanut butter chips over jelly. Stir together reserved crumb mixture with remaining ⅔ cup chips; sprinkle over top.

3. Bake 25 to 30 minutes or until lightly browned. Cool completely in pan on wire rack. Cut into bars.   *Makes about 16 bars*

Tip: For a whimsical twist on this tried-and-true classic, use cookie cutters to cut out shapes for added fun.

Jiggly Banana Split

3 gelatin snack cups (3 ounces each), any flavors
1 banana
3 tablespoons whipped topping
   Colored sprinkles
1 maraschino cherry

1. Unmold snack cups by dipping partially in warm water for a few seconds. Slide gelatin from cups into center of serving dish.

2. Peel banana and cut in half lengthwise. Place banana slices on each side of gelatin.

3. Top with dollops of whipped topping, sprinkles and cherry.

Makes 1 serving

Peanut Butter Chips and Jelly Bars

Cookie Caterpillars

Easy All-Purpose Cookie Dough (recipe follows)
1 cup chocolate hazelnut spread
White chocolate chips, decors, red licorice strings and
    candy-coated chocolate pieces

1. Prepare Easy All-Purpose Cookie Dough.

2. Preheat oven to 300°F. Roll out dough between two sheets of plastic wrap to ¼-inch thickness. Cut out circles with 1¼-inch round cookie cutter. Place 1 inch apart on ungreased cookie sheets.

3. Bake 12 to 15 minutes or until tops of cookies are dry to the touch. Cool on cookie sheets 1 minute. Remove to wire racks; cool completely.

4. Assemble caterpillars by attaching 7 or 8 cookies together, using chocolate hazelnut spread as "glue" between cookies. Create faces, antennae and legs on caterpillars with chocolate chips, decors, licorice strings and candies. *Makes 12 caterpillars*

Easy All-Purpose Cookie Dough

1 cup (2 sticks) butter, softened
½ cup powdered sugar
2 tablespoons packed light brown sugar
¼ teaspoon salt
¼ cup unsweetened Dutch process cocoa powder
1 egg
2 cups all-purpose flour

1. Beat butter, powdered sugar, brown sugar and salt in large bowl with electric mixer at medium speed 2 minutes or until light and fluffy. Add cocoa and egg; beat until well blended.

2. Add flour, ½ cup at a time, beating well after each addition. Shape dough into disc; wrap tightly in plastic wrap. Refrigerate at least 1 hour or until firm.

Cookie Caterpillars

Cookie Dough Bears

1 package (about 18 ounces) refrigerated sugar cookie dough
1 cup uncooked quick oats
   Mini semisweet chocolate chips

1. Combine cookie dough and oats in medium bowl; mix well. Cover and freeze 15 minutes.

2. Preheat oven to 350°F. Lightly spray cookie sheets with nonstick cooking spray. For each bear, shape 1 (1-inch) ball for body and 1 (¾-inch) ball for head. Place body and head together on cookie sheet; flatten slightly. Form 7 small balls for arms, legs, ears and nose; arrange on bear body and head. Place 2 chocolate chips on each head for eyes. Place 1 chocolate chip on each body for belly button.

3. Bake 12 to 14 minutes or until edges are lightly browned. Cool bears on cookie sheets 2 minutes. Remove to wire racks; cool completely.   *Makes about 9 bears*

Editor's Note

This recipe is one of our favorites! Refrigerated cookie dough makes preparation quick and easy, plus kids get to help roll the dough and shape it into bears. And what kid doesn't like to play with dough?

Hershey®'s Milk Chocolate Chip Giant Cookies

6 tablespoons butter, softened
½ cup granulated sugar
¼ cup packed light brown sugar
½ teaspoon vanilla extract
1 egg
1 cup all-purpose flour
½ teaspoon baking soda
2 cups (11.5-ounce package) HERSHEY®'S Milk Chocolate Chips
Frosting (optional)
Ice cream (optional)

1. Heat oven to 350°F. Line two 9-inch round baking pans with foil, extending foil over edges of pans.

2. Beat butter, granulated sugar, brown sugar and vanilla until fluffy. Add egg; beat well. Stir together flour and baking soda; gradually add to butter mixture, beating until well blended. Stir in milk chocolate chips. Spread one half of batter in each prepared pan, spreading to 1 inch from edge. (Cookies will spread to edge when baking.)

3. Bake 18 to 22 minutes or until lightly browned.* Cool completely; carefully lift cookies from pans and remove foil. Frost, if desired. Cut each cookie into wedges; serve topped with scoop of ice cream, if desired.   *Makes about 12 to 16 servings*

*Bake cookies on the middle rack of the oven, one pan at a time. Uneven browning can occur if baking on more than one rack at the same time.

Ice Cream Sandwiches

1 package (about 18 ounces) chocolate cake mix with pudding
    in the mix
2 eggs
¼ cup warm water
3 tablespoons butter, melted
2 cups vanilla ice cream, softened
    Colored sugars or sprinkles

1. Preheat oven to 350°F. Line 13×9-inch baking pan with foil; spray
with nonstick cooking spray.

2. Beat cake mix, eggs, water and butter in large bowl with electric
mixer until well blended. (Dough will be thick and sticky.) Press
dough evenly into prepared pan; prick surface evenly with fork (about
40 times).

3. Bake 20 minutes or until toothpick inserted into center comes out
clean. Cool in pan on wire rack.

4. Cut cookie in half crosswise; remove one half from pan. Spread ice
cream evenly over cookie half remaining in pan. Top with second half;
use foil in pan to wrap up sandwich.

5. Freeze at least 4 hours. Cut into 8 equal pieces; dip sides in sugar
or sprinkles. Wrap sandwiches and freeze until ready to serve.

Makes 8 sandwiches

Note: If the ice cream is too hard to scoop easily, microwave on HIGH
10 seconds to soften.

Peppermint Ice Cream Sandwiches: Stir ⅓ cup crushed peppermint
candies into vanilla ice cream before assembling. Roll ends of
sandwiches in additional crushed peppermint candies to coat.

Blueberry Muffin Bread Pudding

1 tablespoon butter, melted
1½ cups milk
2 eggs
4 (2-ounce) packages miniature blueberry muffins

1. Preheat oven to 350°F. Brush four 6-ounce ramekins with melted butter.

2. Whisk together milk and eggs in medium bowl. Add muffins; toss to coat well. Let stand 15 minutes to allow muffins to absorb milk mixture.

3. Spoon mixture into prepared ramekins. Bake 15 minutes or until lightly browned on top. *Makes 4 servings*

Serving Suggestion: Would be great with a dollop of whipped cream and fresh blueberries.

Brownie Gems

1 package DUNCAN HINES® Chocolate Lover's® Double Fudge Brownie Mix
2 eggs
2 tablespoons water
⅓ cup vegetable oil
28 miniature peanut butter cups or chocolate kiss candies
1 container of your favorite Duncan Hines frosting

1. Preheat oven to 350°F. Spray (1¾-inch) mini muffin pans with vegetable cooking spray or line with foil baking cups.

2. Combine brownie mix, fudge packet from mix, eggs, water and oil in large bowl. Stir with spoon until well blended, about 50 strokes. Drop 1 heaping teaspoonful of batter into each muffin cup; top with candy. Cover candy with more batter. Bake at 350°F for 15 to 17 minutes.

3. Cool 5 minutes. Carefully loosen brownies from pan. Remove to wire racks to cool completely. Frost and decorate as desired.

Makes 30 brownie gems

Blueberry Muffin Bread Pudding

Giggle Jiggle Parfaits

3 envelopes unflavored gelatin
1½ cups water
¾ cup frozen pineapple-orange-apple juice concentrate or passion
    fruit juice concentrate (about ½ of 11½-ounce can)
    Food coloring (optional)
3 cups mixed fresh berries (blueberries, blackberries and/or
    raspberries)
2 containers (6 ounces each) orange cream or lemon yogurt

1. Spray 8-inch square baking dish with nonstick cooking spray.
Sprinkle gelatin over water in small saucepan; let stand 5 minutes.

2. Cook and stir gelatin mixture over medium heat until boiling.
Remove from heat; stir in juice concentrate and food coloring, if
desired, until concentrate melts. Pour into prepared baking dish. Cover
and refrigerate about 4 hours or until firm.

3. Use 1- to 1½-inch cookie cutters to cut gelatin mixture into shapes.
Remove shapes from baking dish.

4. Layer gelatin shapes, berries and yogurt alternately in 6 parfait
glasses. Serve immediately.   *Makes 6 servings*

Prep Time: 15 minutes • **Chill Time:** 4 hours

Kitchen Tip

To make the remaining pineapple-orange-apple
juice concentrate into juice, measure the amount
of remaining concentrate (about 5¾ ounces) and
then add 3 times that amount in water (about
2 cups, 2 tablespoons and 2 teaspoons). Stir
well and enjoy!

Giggle Jiggle Parfaits

S'mores with an Oatmeal Twist

8 large oatmeal cookies
½ thin chocolate candy bar, broken into squares
1 medium ripe banana, cut into 8 slices
4 large marshmallows

1. Place four cookies flat side up on serving plate. Top each cookie with 2 chocolate squares and 2 banana slices.

2. Toast marshmallows;* place on top of banana slices. Top with remaining cookies, flat side down. Serve immediately.

Makes 4 servings

To toast marshmallows, place on a skewer and hold over low flame of gas stove, rotating to toast all sides.

S'mores with a Ginger Twist: Substitute ginger cookies for the oatmeal cookies and fresh peaches or apricot slices for the banana.

Chocolate Peanut Butter Cookies

1 package DUNCAN HINES® Moist Deluxe® Devil's Food Cake Mix
¾ cup crunchy peanut butter
2 eggs
2 tablespoons milk
1 cup candy-coated peanut butter pieces*

You may use 1 cup peanut butter chips in place of peanut butter pieces.

1. Preheat oven to 350°F. Grease baking sheets.

2. Combine cake mix, peanut butter, eggs and milk in large mixing bowl. Beat at low speed with electric mixer until blended. Stir in peanut butter pieces.

3. Drop dough by slightly rounded tablespoonfuls onto prepared baking sheets. Bake 7 to 9 minutes or until lightly browned. Cool 2 minutes on baking sheets. Remove to cooling racks. Cool completely. Store in airtight container.

Makes about 3½ dozen cookies

S'mores with an Oatmeal Twist

Cookie Sundae Cups

1 package (about 16 ounces) refrigerated chocolate chip cookie
   dough
6 cups (1½ quarts) ice cream, any flavor
Ice cream topping, any flavor
Whipped cream
Colored sprinkles

1. Preheat oven to 350°F. Lightly grease 18 standard (2½-inch) muffin cups.

2. Shape dough into 18 balls; press onto bottoms and up sides of prepared muffin cups.

3. Bake 14 to 18 minutes or until golden brown. Cool in pans on wire racks 10 minutes. Remove to racks; cool completely.

4. Place ⅓ cup ice cream in each cookie cup. Drizzle with ice cream topping. Top with whipped cream and sprinkles.

Makes 1½ dozen cups

Creamy Strawberry-Orange Pops

1 container (8 ounces) strawberry yogurt
¾ cup orange juice
2 teaspoons vanilla
2 cups frozen whole strawberries
2 teaspoons sugar
6 (7-ounce) paper cups
6 wooden sticks

1. Combine yogurt, orange juice and vanilla in food processor or blender. Cover and process until smooth.

2. Add strawberries and sugar. Process until smooth. Pour into 6 paper cups, filling each about three-fourths full. Place in freezer for 1 hour. Insert wooden stick into center of each. Freeze completely. Peel cup off each pop to serve.

Makes 6 servings

Cookie Sundae Cup

Twisty Sticks

1 package (about 16 ounces) refrigerated sugar cookie dough
6 tablespoons all-purpose flour, divided
1 tablespoon unsweetened cocoa powder
2 tablespoons creamy peanut butter
1 cup semisweet chocolate chips
1 tablespoon shortening
   Colored sprinkles and finely chopped peanuts

1. Remove dough from wrapper. Divide dough in half; place in separate medium bowls. Let stand at room temperature about 15 minutes.

2. Add 3 tablespoons flour and cocoa to half of dough; beat with electric mixer at medium speed until well blended. Wrap in plastic wrap; refrigerate at least 1 hour.

3. Add remaining 3 tablespoons flour and peanut butter to remaining half of dough; beat with electric mixer at medium speed until well blended. Wrap in plastic wrap; refrigerate at least 1 hour.

4. Preheat oven to 350°F. Divide chocolate dough into 30 equal pieces. Divide peanut butter dough into 30 equal pieces. Shape each dough piece into 4-inch-long rope on lightly floured surface. For each cookie, twist 1 chocolate rope and 1 peanut butter rope together. Place 2 inches apart on ungreased cookie sheets. Bake 7 to 10 minutes or until set. Remove to wire racks; cool completely.

5. Meanwhile, combine chocolate chips and shortening in small microwavable bowl. Microwave on HIGH 1 minute; stir. Microwave on HIGH for additional 30-second intervals until chips and shortening are completely melted and smooth. Spread chocolate on 1 end of each cookie; top with sprinkles and peanuts as desired. Place on waxed paper. Let stand 30 minutes or until set. *Makes 2½ dozen cookies*

Twisty Sticks

Cookie Pizza Cake

1 package (about 18 ounces) refrigerated chocolate chip cookie
    dough
1 package (about 18 ounces) chocolate cake mix, plus ingredients
    to prepare mix
1 cup prepared vanilla frosting
½ cup peanut butter
1 to 2 tablespoons milk
1 container (16 ounces) chocolate frosting
    Chocolate peanut butter cups, chopped (optional)
    Peanut butter chips (optional)

1. Preheat oven to 350°F. Spray 2 (12×1-inch) round pizza pans with
nonstick cooking spray. Press cookie dough evenly into one pan. Bake
15 to 20 minutes or until edges are golden brown. Cool in pan on wire
rack 20 minutes. Remove from pan; cool completely.

2. Prepare cake mix according to package directions. Fill second
pan one-fourth to half full with batter. (Reserve remaining cake batter
for another use, such as cupcakes.) Bake 10 to 15 minutes or until
toothpick inserted into center comes out clean. Cool in pan on wire
rack 15 minutes. Gently remove cake from pan; cool completely.

3. Combine vanilla frosting and peanut butter in small bowl. Gradually
stir in milk, 1 tablespoon at a time, until mixture is of spreadable
consistency.

4. Place cookie on serving plate. Spread peanut butter frosting over
cookie. Place cake on top of cookie, trimming cookie to match the
size of cake, if necessary. Frost top and side of cake with chocolate
frosting. Garnish with peanut butter cups and peanut butter chips.

Makes 12 to 14 servings

Cookie Pizza Cake

The publisher would like to thank the companies and organizations listed below for the use of their recipes and photographs in this publication.

Courtesy of The Beef Checkoff

Campbell Soup Company

Cream of Wheat® Cereal

Duncan Hines® and Moist Deluxe® are registered trademarks of Pinnacle Foods Corp.

The Hershey Company

Nestlé USA

Reckitt Benckiser Inc.

Unilever

VOLUME MEASUREMENTS (dry)

$1/8$ teaspoon = 0.5 mL
$1/4$ teaspoon = 1 mL
$1/2$ teaspoon = 2 mL
$3/4$ teaspoon = 4 mL
1 teaspoon = 5 mL
1 tablespoon = 15 mL
2 tablespoons = 30 mL
$1/4$ cup = 60 mL
$1/3$ cup = 75 mL
$1/2$ cup = 125 mL
$2/3$ cup = 150 mL
$3/4$ cup = 175 mL
1 cup = 250 mL
2 cups = 1 pint = 500 mL
3 cups = 750 mL
4 cups = 1 quart = 1 L

VOLUME MEASUREMENTS (fluid)

1 fluid ounce (2 tablespoons) = 30 mL
4 fluid ounces ($1/2$ cup) = 125 mL
8 fluid ounces (1 cup) = 250 mL
12 fluid ounces ($1 1/2$ cups) = 375 mL
16 fluid ounces (2 cups) = 500 mL

WEIGHTS (mass)

$1/2$ ounce = 15 g
1 ounce = 30 g
3 ounces = 90 g
4 ounces = 120 g
8 ounces = 225 g
10 ounces = 285 g
12 ounces = 360 g
16 ounces = 1 pound = 450 g

DIMENSIONS

$1/16$ inch = 2 mm
$1/8$ inch = 3 mm
$1/4$ inch = 6 mm
$1/2$ inch = 1.5 cm
$3/4$ inch = 2 cm
1 inch = 2.5 cm

OVEN TEMPERATURES

250°F = 120°C
275°F = 140°C
300°F = 150°C
325°F = 160°C
350°F = 180°C
375°F = 190°C
400°F = 200°C
425°F = 220°C
450°F = 230°C

BAKING PAN SIZES

Utensil	Size in Inches/Quarts	Metric Volume	Size in Centimeters
Baking or Cake Pan (square or rectangular)	$8 \times 8 \times 2$	2 L	$20 \times 20 \times 5$
	$9 \times 9 \times 2$	2.5 L	$23 \times 23 \times 5$
	$12 \times 8 \times 2$	3 L	$30 \times 20 \times 5$
	$13 \times 9 \times 2$	3.5 L	$33 \times 23 \times 5$
Loaf Pan	$8 \times 4 \times 3$	1.5 L	$20 \times 10 \times 7$
	$9 \times 5 \times 3$	2 L	$23 \times 13 \times 7$
Round Layer Cake Pan	$8 \times 1 1/2$	1.2 L	20×4
	$9 \times 1 1/2$	1.5 L	23×4
Pie Plate	$8 \times 1 1/4$	750 mL	20×3
	$9 \times 1 1/4$	1 L	23×3
Baking Dish or Casserole	1 quart	1 L	—
	$1 1/2$ quart	1.5 L	—
	2 quart	2 L	—